God's Guide for Work: Discovering God's Will for a Particular Job

The Education of Labor in the Bible

Bible Sermons

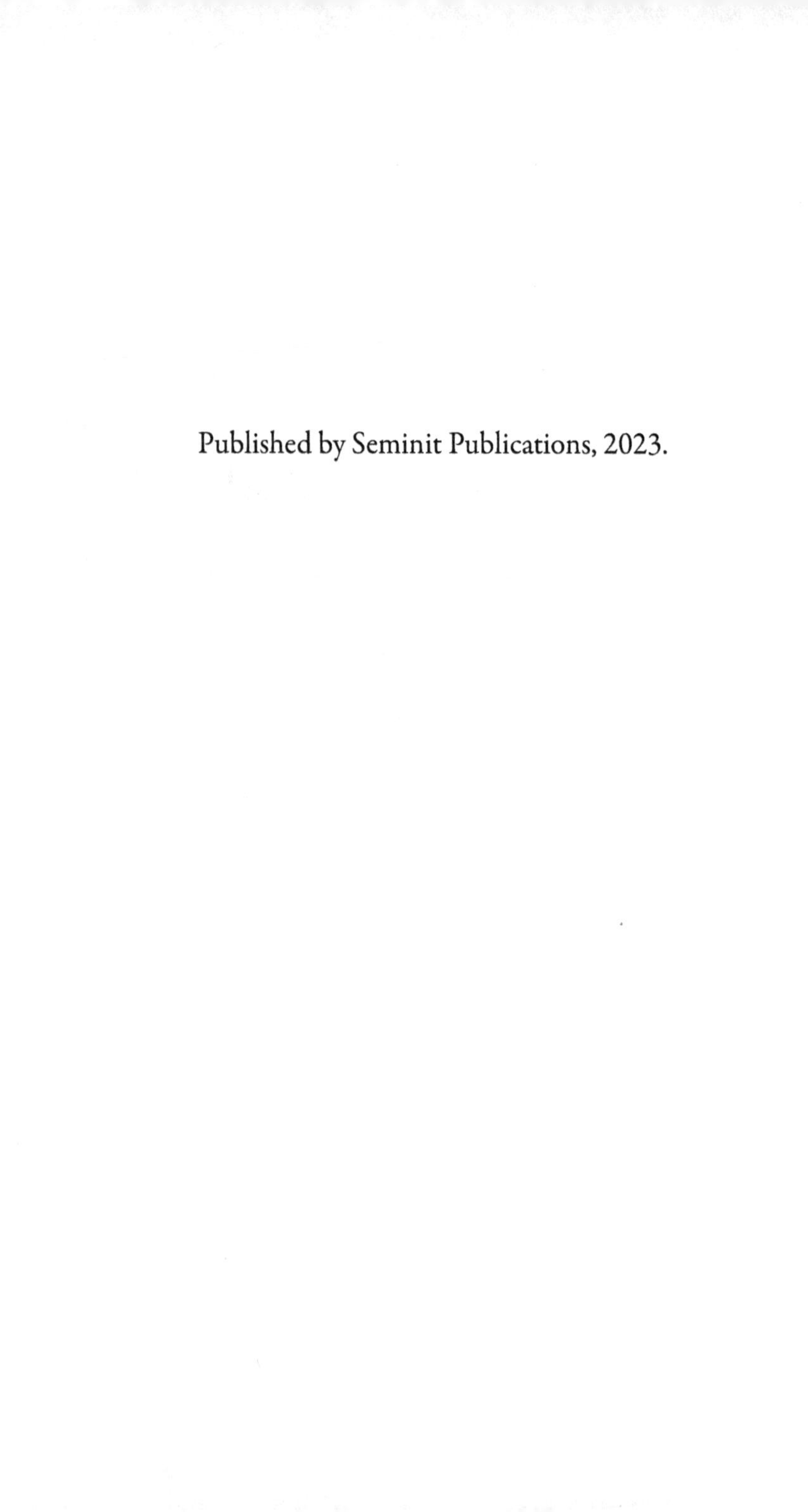

Published by Seminit Publications, 2023.

While every precaution has been taken in the preparation of this book, the publisher assumes no responsibility for errors or omissions, or for damages resulting from the use of the information contained herein.

GOD'S GUIDE FOR WORK: DISCOVERING GOD'S WILL FOR A PARTICULAR JOB

First edition. March 30, 2023.

Copyright © 2023 Bible Sermons.

Written by Bible Sermons.

Table of Contents

Dedication

Proverbs 27:18. *He that keepeth the fig tree shall eat of the fruit thereof: and he that waiteth for his lord shall be honored. As in water the face responds to the face, so the heart of man to man.*

If I look into the water, I see the reflection of my own face, not another man's; and if I look into society, I shall probably see men of like mind to my own. How is it that a drunkard always discovers drunks? How is it that lewd men always have a bad opinion of the morality of others? How is it that hypocrites always think other people are hypocrites? Why, because they can see the reflection of their own faces. When a man tells me there is no love in the Church of God, I know it is because he sees his own face and knows there is no love in it. You will generally find that men measure other people's corn with their own bushels. They are sure to deal out to others according to their own measure; and so they unconsciously betray themselves.

— **Charles Spurgeon**

Introduction

When Christians ask about calling, we often mean, "Is God calling me? Is there a specific job, career or type of work?". This is an important question because the work we do is important to God. If the work is important, it makes sense to ask what work God wants us to do.

In the Bible, God calls people, at least some, to specific jobs, and provides all kinds of guidance in their jobs. So, as a preliminary answer, we can say "yes". God directs people to certain jobs, occupations and types of jobs. But in the Bible, the concept of calling goes beyond any particular aspect of life. God calls people to join him in every area of life. This can only happen in response to Christ's call to follow him. The call to follow Christ is the root of all other calls. However, it is important not to confuse the call to follow Christ with the call to be a professional church worker. People from all walks of life are called to follow Christ with equal depth and commitment.

After analyzing the call to follow Christ, we will analyze the call to specific works in light of many biblical passages related to the call. We will show how the cooperative work of the Trinity of Father, Son and Holy Spirit guides and exemplifies our work. We will provide links for further theological exploration of call. In the process, we will look at related topics such as how to discern God's direction at work, the communal nature of calling, the call to ecclesiastical versus non-ecclesiastical work, calls to God's creative and redemptive work beyond the world of work, the importance of *how we* work in any given area, and the ultimate freedom Christians enjoy in their work environment.

The Different Handling of the Call of God

Invocation to Unite with Christ and Share in His Work of Redemption in the World

---

In the Bible, the word "call" is most often used to refer to belonging to Christ and participating in his redemptive work in the world. This sense of calling is particularly prominent in Paul's letters.

In **Romans 1:6**

...you are also included, whom Jesus Christ has called.

In **Romans 8:28**

God arranges all things for the good of those who love him, those who are called according to his purpose.

In **1 Timothy 2:4**

[God] wants everyone to be saved and to come to know the truth.

In **2 Corinthians 5:17-20**

Therefore, if anyone is in Christ, he is a new creation; the old has passed away, the new has come! All this is from God, who through Christ reconciled us to himself and gave us the ministry of reconciliation: that is, in Christ, God was reconciling the world to himself, not counting its sins against it and entrusting to us the message of reconciliation. So we are Christ's ambassadors, as if God were exhorting you through us: "In the name of Christ we beseech you to be reconciled to God".

The call to belong to Christ goes beyond the type of "calling" in the world of work with which this article is primarily concerned. For this reason, it is important to begin our discussion of the call to follow Jesus. It is a call to a renewed relationship with God, with other people and with the world around us. It encompasses the whole of human being and doing. This reminds us that the call to a particular kind of work is secondary to the call to belong to Christ and participate in his redemption of the world.

In particular, our work must be an essential part of our commitment to Christ himself. His work is the basis for creative and productive acts in the universe (**John 1:1-3**). His redemptive work can occur in every workplace through righteousness, healing, reconciliation, compassion, kindness, humility and patience (**Colossians 3:12**). The work of redemption is not limited to evangelism, but includes everything necessary to make the world what God always intended it to be. This work of redemption is in harmony with the work of creation, production and maintenance entrusted to mankind by God in the Garden of Eden. The Bible does not say that the work of redemption replaced the work of creation. Both continue and, in general, Christians are commanded to participate in the work of creation and redemption.

The Universal Obligation to Labor

———

Before we can discuss the possibility of God's direction to a specific type of work, we must recognize God's *command* for all to work to the extent that they are able. God's command or call to work comes at the very beginning of the Bible, where God chooses to involve human beings in the work of creation, production and sustenance. Work remains until the very end of the Bible. There was work in the Garden of Eden, and there is work in the new heaven and the new earth.

In **Genesis 1:27-28**

And God created man in his own image; he created him in the image of God. Male and female he created them, and blessed them with these words: "Be fruitful and multiply; fill the earth and subdue it; have dominion over the fish of the sea and over the birds of the air, and over all the creeping things that creep along the ground".

In **Genesis 2:15, 19-20**

The Lord God took the man and put him in the garden of Eden to cultivate and care for it... Then the Lord God formed from the ground every bird of the air and every beast of the field, and brought them to the man to see what name he would give them. Man gave names to all living things, and by that name they are known. So man named all the domestic animals, all the birds of the air and all the animals of the field. However, no suitable help for man was found among them.

In **Exodus 20:9**

Work six days, and do in them everything you have to do.

In **2 Thessalonians 3:10**

For even when we were with you, we commanded you, "Whoever does not want to work, let him not eat either".

In **Revelation 21:24-26**

The nations will walk in the light of the city, and the kings of the earth will give it their splendid riches. Its gates shall be open all day long, for there shall be no night there. And they shall bring to it all the riches and honor of the nations.

In **Isaiah 65:21-22**

They shall build houses and inhabit them; they shall plant vineyards and eat their fruit. No longer shall they build houses for others to dwell in, nor plant vineyards for others to eat. For the days of my people shall be as the days of a tree; my chosen ones shall enjoy the works of their hands.

Based on these passages, we can say that everyone is "called" to work, as long as we realize that "called" in this sense really means "sent". God commands you to work, even if He does not give you a specific job offer. In fact, God's command to work can be fulfilled in ways other than paid work. We will discuss God's direction for specific jobs or types of jobs later.

Convocation to Life: Much More than Work

Although we are focusing on God's call to work, work is only one element of life. God calls us to belong to Christ in every element of our lives.

In Colossians 3:17

And whatever you do in word or deed, do it in the name of the Lord Jesus.

Our work is not necessarily the most important aspect of our calling or service in Christ's redemptive work. First, we must remember that work is not limited to paid work. The work God directs us to do may be unpaid work, such as raising children or caring for disabled family members or tutoring students after school. God may not call many of us to paid work that completely prevents us from doing unpaid work.

Even if you have a paying job, the main work God has called you to do may be outside of your job. The job may satisfy your need for money, which in itself makes it part of God's ordained work, but it may fail to fulfill all of God's other purposes for your life. We have seen that caring for children and caring for the elderly or disabled is work, and many of the people who do it have other paying jobs. On the other hand, so-called hobbies can be work that God leads you to do, instead of your paid work. You can work in literature, painting, music, acting, astronomy, leading a youth group, volunteering at a historical society, maintaining a nature preserve, or a thousand other jobs. If something like this is your vocation, you are likely to take it more seriously than someone who sees it as a leisure activity. There is a difference between work and play. But any given activity, paid or unpaid, is work to one person and play to another.

Second, we must be careful not to let work dominate other elements of our life. Even if God has led you to a particular job or career, you must set boundaries for that work in order to leave room for other elements of God's calling or direction in your life. For example, if God has led you to marry and have a small business, you will need to balance the time and responsibilities of these two callings. Work should not replace leisure, rest and worship. There is no formula for balancing work and other elements of life. But be careful not to let a sense of calling to work blind you to God's call in other areas of your life.

Divine Guidance for a Specific Task

At this point, we can now delve deeper into the possibility of God's direction for a particular task, job, occupation or type of work. We have seen:

All are called to belong to Christ and to participate in his work of creation and redemption.

2. It is unusual for God to call someone directly and unequivocally to a certain work.

Everyone is sent to work to the best of their ability, but God usually does not provide specific job opportunities.

4. God calls us to live a full life, not just a job.

Putting these four points together, we can conclude that your career is not what matters most to God. If it is, he will call you directly and unequivocally. Furthermore, what God values most is that you work according to his words, come to Christ's redeeming grace, and participate in his work of creation and redemption. The specific type of work you do is less important.

While God's primary concern is not to get us the right job or career, that doesn't mean he doesn't care. In fact, the distinctive work of the Holy Spirit is to guide and equip people to live and work as God has shown them. In the Old Testament, God sometimes gave people the skills needed for their jobs, as we saw in the examples of Bezalel and Aholiab. But now the Holy Spirit usually guides believers in specific jobs and gives them the skills they need (**1 Corinthians 12:7-12**). He gives guidance on what kind of work people do and how to do it.

Discovering Divine Guidance for a Determined Job Role

Invoking the Right Work: A Clear and Unequivocal Appeal

Knowing that the ultimate picture of calling in the Bible is the call to follow Jesus, we are ready to explore calling to specific types of work. If by "calling" we mean a direct and unequivocal command from God to undertake a particular task, job, occupation, or type of work, then calling is very rare in the Bible. In this sense, there are no more than a hundred people who are called by God. God called Noah to build the ark. God called Moses and Aaron to his mission (Exodus 3:4, 28:1). He called prophets such as Samuel (1 Samuel 3:10), Jeremiah (Jeremiah 1:4-5), Amos (Amos 7:15), etc. He calls Abraham and Sarah and several others to travel or move (which could be considered a workplace call). He appointed men to serve as political leaders, including Joseph, Gideon, Saul, David, and David's descendants. God chose Bezalel and Aholiab to be the master craftsmen of the Tabernacle (Exodus 31:1-6). Jesus called the apostles and some of his other disciples (e.g., Mark 3:14-19), and the Holy Spirit called Barnabas and Saul to be missionaries (Acts 13:2). The word "called" is not always used, but in these cases it is clear that God is unequivocally directing specific people to specific tasks.

Apart from these, there are very few people in the Bible who accept a personal call from God. This strongly suggests that a direct call from God to a specific job is also very rare today. If God has called you directly and unequivocally to a particular job, you do not need the guidance of articles like this, except confirmation, and yes, such a call is rare in the Bible. So, instead of looking further into the direct and unmistakable personal call, we focus on whether God guides or directs people to specific types of work in less dramatic ways.

Guide to find your career

While God does not give most people an immediate, personal and unequivocal call to a particular job or vocation, God leads people in less dramatic ways, including Bible study, prayer, Christian community and personal church reflection. Cultivating a general awareness of God's direction in life is beyond the scope of this article. But we will look at three important considerations for discerning God's career direction.

First things first. Probably the strongest indicator of what God wants you to do is your awareness of what needs to be done to make the world more like God wants it to be. It doesn't necessarily mean a big world problem, but anything that needs to be done in the world. Earning a living to support yourself and your family is an example mentioned in the Bible:

In **Proverbs 13:22**

A good man leaves an inheritance to his grandchildren.

In **Proverbs 14:1**

A wise woman builds her house, but a foolish woman destroys it with her hands.

In **1 Timothy 5:8**

He who does not provide for his own, and especially for those of his own household, has denied the faith and is worse than an unbeliever.

In **Titus 3:14**

May our people learn to strive to do good works, so that they may attend to what is really necessary and not lead a useless life.

Another biblical example is working to meet the needs of people around you besides your family:

In **Proverbs 14:21**

Blessed is he who has pity on the poor!

In **1 Thessalonians 4:11**

Aim to live a quiet life, mind your own business and work with your hands, as we instructed you earlier (NTV).

In **Luke 3:10-11**

"Then what should we do?" the people asked him. "The one who has two shirts should share with the one who has none", John answered them, "and the one who has food should do the same".

In **Proverbs 11:25**

He who is generous prospers; he who revives will be revived.

In **Matthew 25:34-36**

Then the King will say to those on his right hand, "Come, you whom my Father has blessed; receive your inheritance, the kingdom prepared for you since the creation of the world. For I was hungry, and you gave me food; I was thirsty, and you gave me drink; I was a stranger, and you gave me lodging; I needed clothes, and you clothed me; I was sick, and you cared for me; I was in prison, and you visited me".

Working to serve the good of society at large is also a biblical imperative:

In **Jeremiah 29:5-7**

Build houses and dwell in them; plant gardens and eat their fruit. Marry, and bear sons and daughters; and marry your sons and daughters, that they in turn may bear you grandchildren. Multiply there, and do not decrease. Moreover, seek the welfare of the city to which I have deported you, and pray to the Lord for it, for your welfare depends on the welfare of the city.

Of course, you can't meet every need in the world, so you limit yourself somewhat. Start with the needs you are personally responsible for, such as raising children or paying off debts. Beyond that, pay attention to needs that you can meet very well, or that few people are willing to meet, or that you think are particularly urgent. For example, you may be better prepared to apply for a position in your own city or town than to move to find a job. On the other hand, you may be one of the few willing to document human rights violations in a country halfway around the world. Or you may be convinced that teaching troubled youth is more urgent than joining a gang. Also, it may become clear to you that certain things in your life, besides your job or career, are the most important ways in which you help you feel fulfilled. It doesn't make sense to get a job counseling troubled youth while neglecting your own children.

The point is that God has given each individual the ability to know a part of the world that they need. He was apparently waiting for us to feel and get to work, not because of his special calling. There is no biblical formula that translates into precise job requirements. That is why you should seek God's guidance in the variety of discernment available to you.

The second consideration is their abilities and gifts. The bible says that God gives gifts to people to do the work He wants them to do, it mentions some of the gifts and abilities that God gives:

In **Isaiah 28:24-26**

When a farmer plows for sowing, does he plow without rest? Does he spend every day breaking and raking his ground? After he has evened the surface, does he not sow dill and scatter cummin? Does he not sow wheat in rows, barley in the proper place, and rye on the borders? It is God who instructs him and teaches him how to do it.

In **Romans 12:6-8**

We have different gifts, according to the grace given to us. If someone's gift is that of prophecy, let him use it in proportion to his faith; if it is that of rendering service, let him render it; if it is that of teaching, let him teach; if it is that of encouraging others, let him encourage them; if it is that of succoring the needy, let him give

*generously; if it is that of leading, let him lead with care; if it is that
of showing compassion, let him do it with joy.*

In **1 Corinthians 12:7-10**

*To each is given a special manifestation of the Spirit for the good
of others. To some God gives by the Spirit the word of wisdom; to
others, by the same Spirit, the word of knowledge; to others, faith
through the same Spirit; to others, and by that same Spirit, gifts
to heal the sick; to others, miraculous powers; to others, prophecy;
to others, the discerning of spirits; to others, speaking in various
languages; and to others, the interpretation of tongues.*

As the last two passages show, when Paul speaks of the gifts of
the Holy Spirit, he is usually referring to their use in the church.
But if all the work that Christians do is for the Lord (**Colossians
3:23**), then we can infer that the gift of the Holy Spirit is also
given for use in the workplace. Thus, gifts and abilities provide
an element of direction to discern God's leading.

A number of tools have been developed to help people identify
their gifts and use them in the workplace (see 'Explore more').
However, it is easy to focus too much on one's own skills and
talents. The current generation of Westerners is the most
scrutinized genius in human history, but this love of scrutiny can
lead to self-absorption and distraction from these scriptures that
say God gives gifts for the common good, not for satisfaction.
Also, in many cases, God gives gifts to a person only after he has
done the work he needs to do. Focusing too much on the gifts
you already have can prevent you from receiving the gifts God
wants for you.

However, the gifts you already have can tell you the best way to find yourself. It would be narcissistic to claim that God called you to be the world's greatest pianist and then expect him to infuse you with the necessary talent after years of mediocre piano playing and poor practice. Career direction through skills and gifts is a difficult balancing act, so it must be sought in a relationship with God and fellow Christians.

Here again, we emphasize that we should not concentrate on work and neglect the rest of our lives. God also gives us gifts for family life, friendship, recreation, volunteering and all of life's activities.

Finally, the Bible says that your truest or deepest desires also matter to God.

In **Psalm 37:4**

Delight yourself in the Lord, and he will give you the desires of your heart.

In **Psalm 145:19**

He fulfills the desires of those who fear him; he hears their cry and saves them.

In **Matthew 5:6**

Blessed are those who hunger and thirst for righteousness, for they shall be satisfied.

In **John 16:24**

Until now you have asked for nothing in my name. Ask and you will receive, so that your joy may be complete.

Sometimes Christians hope that if God calls them to a job, it will be something they hate. Otherwise, why would God call them? A sick Christian fantasy is to imagine a country you'd rather not live in and then assume that God has called you to be a missionary there. But the best missionaries have a burning desire for the place and the people they serve. Besides, who said God wanted you to be a missionary? If God has led you to a certain job or career, you are more likely to find a deep-seated desire for it.

However, it can be very difficult to connect with your truest or deepest desires. Our motives are so confused by sin and the deterioration of the world that our surface desires are often far removed from the real desires God has implanted deep within us.

In **Romans 7:8, 15, 21-23**

But sin, taking advantage of the opportunity provided by the commandment, awakened in me every kind of covetousness. For apart from the law sin is dead... I do not understand what happens to me, for I do not do what I want, but what I abhor... So I discover this law: that when I want to do good, evil accompanies me. For in my inmost being I delight in the law of God; but I realize that in the members of my body there is another law, which is the law of sin. This law fights against the law of my mind, and holds me captive.

Therefore, we cannot simply say: "Do what makes you happy". What makes you happy, or what seems to make you happy, may be far from satisfying, or from using your skills and talents for the common good, or even from fulfilling your true desires. Very often the opposite is true, and a job that fulfills your true desires may not seem popular at first glance and may require a great deal of sacrifice and hard work. Your true desires can be fulfilled in many areas of your life, not necessarily at work. Knowing what you really want requires spiritual maturity, which may be more than you may have when faced with a decision. But at least you can escape the idea that God only calls you to do things you hate. With this in mind, Frederick Buechner wrote, "Where God has called you is where your deep joy meets the deep hunger of the world".

These three considerations, your skills and talents, and your truest desires, are guidelines, but they are not absolutes. First, in a fallen world, you probably have little ability to choose your work anyway. Throughout history, most people have worked as slaves, farmers, or housewives, and this is still the case in most of the world. It is hard to imagine, except in some developed countries, that God wants most people to be slaves, farmers or homeowners. Instead, circumstances seem to prevent most people from choosing the jobs they really want to do. This is not to say that some people do not like or should not labor in agriculture, domestic work, or any other type of legitimate work, but the circumstances of the world dictate that many people accept jobs they do not like. However, even being a slave is a blessing under God's care (**Matthew 24:45-47, 1 Corinthians 7:21-24**). This in no way legitimizes slavery in today's world.

It simply means that wherever you work, God is with you. Learning to appreciate the work you have, and finding ways to engage with Christ in that work, may be better than trying to find a job you think you will enjoy more.

Even in advanced economies, many people have few choices in the type of work they do for a living. A Christian community would do a great job of equipping people both to make decisions about their careers and to follow God's lead in whatever work we do. No matter what your job is, God's gift enables you to work for the common good, find more consistency in your work, and overcome or endure the negative aspects of your situation. Most importantly, God promises to ultimately free us from hard work, monotony and thorns.

What about those who have few options and struggle? Can hard, difficult work, a human necessity, be a vocation? Consider, for example, the story of Graeme Marriott, a father of three and foreman at CBM Waste Management:

We are a small company. We have entered the recycling field, but the profit is not very high. Our focus is on waste disposal. My job is to manage the place: I organize and do some paperwork. We collect garbage and recycle... three of us, we start at 3 am.... I did half the run with the compactor and the other half behind the truck. I've been doing it for six years. I take care of recycling every day. It's a lot of physical work. You have to lift things and there's a lot of noise, especially when machining. Running...down steep streets is a physical strain, especially in the summer...you have to start early and it disrupts family life. Work every day, whatever the weather, even on holidays. As an essential service, you can't take time off. I love the physical challenge: how fast and efficient can we be?

But it's a pretty mechanical job: squeezing bottles, chasing trucks.... People ask me what I do and they think I'm lazy. In a sense, this is the last job. But it's essential, and people depend on it. If we go on strike, the garbage starts to pile up, it's a health hazard..... recycling is more important these days, I get a little respect. My daughter's school has me talking to the kids about recycling. These recycling issues affect all of us, so my role is important. I know that even though it's hard to say sometimes, God has called me to do my job.

Graeme's work was hard work, but he made the most of it, shared the difficulties and took his responsibilities seriously as a matter of God's hand.

Even if you have the freedom to choose your work, these three considerations are guides, not dictators. In Christ believers have complete freedom:

In **John 8:36**

If the Son sets you free, you will be truly free.

In **2 Corinthians 3:17**

Now the Lord is the Spirit; and where the Spirit of the Lord is, there is liberty.

This means that you have the freedom to take risks, fail and make mistakes. God may lead you to a job you know nothing about, have no skills for and think you don't like. Would you like to take this job? Instead, later in life, you may neglect God's professional calling for you. Take heart, because in the end you will not be judged for finding the right job or fulfilling your God-given potential. You will be judged according to the merits of Jesus Christ, who has applied to you the grace of God's faith. The call to belong to Christ is the only call that matters.

The body of Christ on earth is the community of believers (**Romans 12:5**). Freedom in Christ means, therefore, that God's call or direction is best discerned in dialogue with the community rather than in isolation. We have seen that (a form of community) is important because you can discern what kind of work God is leading you to do. Community is also an important factor in discerning God's leading. In Acts we read of when Paul and Barnabas were sent on a mission by the church in Antioch (**Acts 13:2-3**), and when Gentiles were received into what was then a predominantly Jewish church AND without onerous burdens, the Holy Spirit guides the Jewish law: "*It is good for the Holy Spirit and for us*" (**Acts 15:28**). This shared discernment, mutual dealing and mutual accountability, is a good model for our professional discernment, although obviously there is also individual freedom and responsibility.

Archbishop William Temple is right that choosing a career for personal or selfish reasons, without a real and collectively affirmed sense of purpose, "is probably the greatest sin any young person can commit, since it includes, most of the time, deliberately misdirecting loyalty and strength from God". But the fault lies, if not greater, with churches that let people go their own way, without the benefit of public discernment and professional guidance, unless they are considering ordained ministry. However, you can proactively call upon your community to help you discern your calling. Ask the following questions of those in your community who know you best: What do others think God has directed you to? What do they see as your talents and abilities, and the deepest desires they see in you? Begin talking about God's leadership with people in your community who know you well. It may be helpful to talk with a partner or spiritual advisor, gather information from the people you work with, or have a group of people meet with you periodically to discern God's direction.

Community is also an essential element in discerning who is being guided to do the different types of work needed in the world. Many people may have similar talents and aspirations, and you can help them realize them. But God probably doesn't want all people to do the same work. You need to discern not only the work God is leading you to do, but also the work He is leading others to do. A community needs a harmonious and balanced whole. Physicians, for example, bring powerful gifts and skills to the world's great need for physical health and, often, a deep desire to heal. However, at least in the United States, there can be too many specialists and not enough primary care physicians to meet the needs of the community. One by one, medical students are matching their talents, aspirations and demanding medical directions. But overall, the healthcare group is a bit unbalanced. Discerning God's call is a community effort.

The Work of the Church: Response to a Divine Invitation?

———

Many Christians have the impression that church workers, especially evangelists, missionaries, pastors, priests, ministers, etc., have a higher calling than other workers. While there is little evidence in the Bible to support this impression, during the Middle Ages, "religious" life, such as that of monks and nuns, was considered more sacred than ordinary life. The monastic tradition exalts "perfect" and contemplative lives, such as Mary's (the Church's) poverty, chastity and obedience, over "permissible" active lives, such as Martha's secular work, marriage and service to society, thus drawing lessons from concrete facts to deduce general principles (**Luke 10:38-42**).

Unfortunately, this distortion still influences all traditional churches, even though the teachings of almost all churches today affirm the equal value of the work of the laity. In the Bible, God calls people to church and non-church related and non-church related jobs:

Quotes Called to Ecclesiastical Work

In **Exodus 28:1**

Bring before you your brother Aaron and his sons Nadab, Abihu, Eleazar, and Ithamar. From among all the Israelites, they shall serve me as priests.

In **Mark 1:16-17**

As Jesus passed by the shore of the Sea of Galilee, he saw Simon and his brother Andrew casting a net into the lake, for they were fishermen. "Come, follow me, "Jesus said to them, "and I will make you fishers of men".

In **Acts 13:2, 5**

While they were fasting and participating in the worship of the Lord, the Holy Spirit said, "Set apart for me now Barnabas and Saul for the work to which I have called them"... When they arrived in Salamis, they preached the word of God in the synagogues of the Jews. They also had John as a helper.

Appointments Called to non-ecclesiastical work

———

In **Deuteronomy 31:14**

The Lord said to Moses, "The day of your death is at hand. Call Joshua, and present yourself with him in the Tent of Meeting, that he may receive my orders". (Moses and Joshua were both fundamentally military/political leaders, not cultic/religious leaders. Both were exceptionally close to God, but that does not make them religious leaders. Rather, this shows that God calls people from all walks of life).

In **1 Samuel 16:12-13**

Isaí sent for him, and they brought him to him. He was handsome, dark, and of good looks. And the Lord said to Samuel, "This is he; arise, anoint him. Samuel took the horn of oil and anointed the young man in the presence of his brothers. Then the Spirit of the Lord came with power upon David, and from that day he was with him. Then Samuel returned to Ramah.

Therefore, the idea that God calls church workers but not other types of workers is inappropriate.

Some confusion arises because many churches require their members to be "called" to be ordained or to serve as pastors, priests or other priests. The word "called" is often used to describe the process of choosing a pastor or deciding to enter full-time church work. However, as in the Bible, these situations are rarely a direct and unequivocal personal call from God. Instead, they may describe a strong sense of direction from God. As we have seen, God's direction occurs with equal force in jobs and occupations outside the church. Since we do not include church work as one of its themes, we will not attempt to evaluate whether the "call" to church work is stronger, more immediate, more obvious, or more necessary than the call to work outside the church. We wish to affirm that church work in general is not a higher calling than work outside the church, and that the term "calling" applies equally to work outside the church as to church work.

We also affirm that work outside the church is "full-time Christian service" just like church work. All Christians are called (i.e., ordained) to do whatever they do for Christ 24 hours a day:

In **Colossians 3:23**

Whatever you do, work willingly, as for the Lord and not as for anyone else in this world.

Before concluding our discussion on this point, we should note that one school of thought holds that 1 Timothy 5:17-18 contradicts what we have described. According to this view, becoming an elder of a church (often equivalent to the pastor or shepherd used by modern churches) is actually a higher calling.

In **1 Timothy 5:17-18**

Elders who conduct the affairs of the church well are worthy of double honor, especially those who devote their efforts to preaching and teaching. For the Scripture says: "Do not muzzle the ox while he is threshing", and "The laborer deserves to be paid his wages".

According to this office, being a priest is a "double honor" in relation to other professions. But most reviews reject this explanation. A more appropriate reading would be that elders who do a good job deserve double the honor (or honor) compared to elders who do a good job. Or, a contrast may arise between elders who volunteer part-time and elders who work full-time for the church. The quotes in the Old Testament about compensation further reinforce the idea that this passage is about rewarding high performers or staff elders rather than comparing church work to other types of work. This means that elders who work full time for the church and do a good job should be adequately paid by the church. The real comparison in this passage is between pastors, not between pastors and laity.

The only works that do not have equal status in the eyes of God are those that require a biblical prohibition or are incompatible with his values. For example, murder, adultery, theft, false witness or greed (**Exodus 20:13-17**), usury (**Leviticus 25:26**), damage to health (**Matthew 10:8**), or damage to the environment (**Genesis 2: 15**) is not lawful before God. This is not to say that those who do these jobs are of lesser status in the eyes of God. People whose circumstances lead them to work illegally are not illegal. In some cases, such jobs may be the lesser of two evils, but they are by no means the jobs intended by God for anyone.

Looking for a New Job

I f God directs or guides people to do His work, is it legal to change jobs? Wouldn't that be a rejection of God's direction for the job you already have? The 16th century Protestant theologian Martin Luther made a famous case against changing jobs. This is based primarily on his understanding of the passage:

In **1 Corinthians 7:20**

May each one remain in the condition [klesei] in which he was when God called him.

But many today say that Luther's position on the calling of an individual to a social or professional role was due to his mistranslation of the Greek word *klesei* in **1 Corinthians 7:20** as "*vocation*" or "*calling*" in the vocational sense. This influenced the King James Bible, which says that every man obeys the calling God has given him. Contrast this with the more liberal modern translation: "*Let every man remain in the state in which God has called him*" (NIV) or conversion.

Luther's contemporary, John Calvin, did not accept Luther's interpretation, nor do most modern theologians. At first glance, it does not seem to adequately explain the following verses, which suggest that career changes are legitimate, at least in some cases:

In **1 Corinthians 7:21**

Were you a slave when you were called? Don't worry, though, if you have the opportunity to get your freedom, take advantage of it.

In choosing between these two positions, we must remember that this passage refers to marriage, not career. The Corinthians' desire to ascend socially and spiritually led them to question Paul's question about marriage, and they were trying to make the transition to an ostensibly more spiritual and heavenly state of singleness (**1 Corinthians 7:1**). In response, Paul reiterated his general principle of maintaining the same status/class and role in which they became. After all, Christ is there to call them or convert them, thus making their social roles relative rather than absolute. The difference is calling a situation (Calvin) and calling a situation (Luther) into conversion. Os Guinness captures the meaning of our original calling: "*First, we are called to someone (God), not to something (such as motherhood, politics or teaching) or to a place (such as a slum or Mongolia)*".

However, while God's call to conversion and Christian conduct is not identical to these social spheres, it is intimately related to them and sanctifies them. In any case, the use of call language for relationships and work roles is justified, as Fee points out:

What Paul is saying is that by calling a person to a particular situation, that very situation will be present in the call, thus sanctifying him. Likewise, in saving a person in that situation, Christ "appoints" them to be his place to live in Christ...precisely because our lives are determined by God's calling, not by our circumstances that dictate that we need to learn to continue to be there as one who "before God..". We are there to serve the

Lord... whether in interracial marriages, singles, work or office jobs, or socioeconomic status.

Paul then compares salvation by circumcision (**1 Corinthians 7:18-19**) and slavery/occupation (**1 Corinthians 7:21-24; cf. Galatians 3:28**). However, unlike the Corinthian position that our professional relationship/environment is just a stage or scaffolding to be discarded as soon as possible, Paul sees this as an underlying part of our primary calling to live out our salvation in life. Secondary social and occupational roles. Like the sacraments, callings are outward and visible signs of inner spiritual transformation.

For Paul, our relationship and professional environment was not casual, but providential. Stay in the situation in which you were called or converted, even the most desperate situation has the potential to be transformed into a place of service to God. But this is not a hard and fast rule. Paul argues that a change of occupation or role is undesirable in some circumstances, e.g., selling as a slave or changing racial identity (uncircumcision); and unnecessary but possible or desirable in others, e.g., if a slave owner or non-Christian spouse is permitted. a freedom (**1 Corinthians 7:15, 21**).

Therefore, the Corinthians did not need to abandon their social roles or remain in them. Paul's interpretation of **1 Corinthians 7:29-31** highlights the pressures on Christian freedom in marriage and work in a fallen world between the present and the future Kingdom of God. *We do not have much time left. From now on, those who have wives must live as if they had no wives...* *"those who buy things must act as if they have nothing; those who* *enjoy worldly things".* things do not seem to enjoy them; that is why the world, in its present form, is about to disappear. We are called to remain in our earthly situation/function or creation, but our allegiance and primary concerns are called to withdraw to the new creation.

Luther emphasized the permanence of his calling while living through the distortions created by a thousand years of monastic denial of marriage and secular life. 500 years later, Miroslav Volf emphasized the withdrawn aspect when Luther's own teachings were twisted into a "Protestant work ethic" in which work became the primary calling, and even the source of salvation. In response to these two distortions, the spirit of new creation transforms our social and working conditions, making the gift flourish.

In summary, Paul challenges the Corinthians and us to maintain our availability to the kingdom of God or the new creation, but not to give up the created role that that kingdom will preserve and perfect. Despite the tension between our roles in creation and the kingdom of God (**1 Corinthians 7:29-31**), there is a tension between being called to stay and being called to go, both of which were reconciled in the end because the kingdom was "created and healed".

Recently, Miroslav Volf wrote that God can certainly lead people to change jobs because the factors that lead them to work can change over the course of a working life. Your skills should grow with your experience in serving God. He can lead you through more important tasks that require you to change jobs. *"Well have you done, good and faithful servant! You have been faithful to a point; I will hold you accountable for more. Come and share in the joy of your master!"* (**Matthew 25:21**).

On the other hand, if you become a Christian as an adult, will God ask you to change jobs? Finding a new life in Christ may seem like finding a new job or career. However, this is usually not the case. Since there are no career hierarchies, it is often a mistake to think that God wants you to find a "superior career" by becoming a Christian. Unless your job is of the illegal type we discussed above, or unless the job or co-workers threaten to trap you in un-Christian habits, it may not be necessary to change jobs. However, whether you change jobs or not, your job may need to be different and focus on biblical commandments, values and virtues now, just as Zacchaeus, the tax collector, did:

In **Luke 19:5-9**

Arriving at the place, Jesus looked up and said to him, "Zacchaeus, come down at once. I have to stay at your house today. So he hurried down and, overjoyed, received Jesus into his house. When they saw this, they all began to murmur, "He has gone to stay with a sinner. But Zacchaeus said resolutely, "Look, Lord, right now I am going to give half of my goods to the poor, and if I have defrauded anyone of anything, I will repay him four times as much". "Today salvation has come to this house", Jesus said to him, "for this man also is a son of Abraham.

Identifying the Divine Purpose for Your Work

We have suggested many times that the way you work is at least as important to God as your job or career. In every job we have at least some opportunity to meet people's needs, develop our gifts and skills, and express, or discover, our deepest desires. Your daily decisions to serve God today are more important than positioning yourself for the right job tomorrow. In fact, the little you can do today in God's service is often the key to being able to do more in the future. "*He who is honest in small things will be honest in great things*", Jesus said (**Luke 16:10**). Throughout your life, you can best serve Christ by using every job to fulfill His purpose, whether or not you feel called to each job.

Conclusion

We take into account the call and direction of God for those who are engaged in a variety of ordinary work. By this we are trying to correct the old Protestant tendency that ordinary work is irrelevant to God and unworthy of His calling. But it is equally wrong to elevate the importance of your job or career to the status of idolatry. Finding the right job does not bring salvation, or even happiness. Moreover, the true purpose of Christian work is to serve the public good, not to promote one's own. In your life, serve the common good more by doing your daily work to the best of your ability in Christ than by finding the best job for yourself.

In Gail Godwin's novel <u>Evesong</u>, one character reiterates his mission by telling another, "If something always makes you better, then it's your calling". It's not just a job, it's part of a "faithful and prosperous life". Although today the language of passion pervades everything, including careers, it is not just passion in the emotional sense. It is the commitment and disciplined practice of a lifelong focus, not a "bite-sized" approach to food or a "quickie" approach to media. It is this that "always makes you better". In this way, vocations or callings are linked to long-term holistic covenants related to the responsibilities of our roles as husbands and wives, parents and children, bosses and workers, rulers and citizens, with our closest neighbors. Godwin's view helps guide us toward careers that promote life flourishing.

Gregory Jones added to Godwin: "Instead, we should avoid those occupations that may make us 'worse,' especially if we are engaged in occupations in which we may be punished by sin in some 'withering' way or other. It is possible to become 'worse' because of our own temptations, a peculiar incompatibility between what we do and the gift God has given us, an accident that kills the possibility of continuing a certain profession or practice, or The corrupt institutions that presently shape our profession".

But Goodwin's saying "make yourself better" can be absorbed into the seductive culture of self-realization. It should be compared to Dietrich Bonhoeffer's saying in The Cost of Cicipleship that "when Christ calls [someone], he commands him to come and die", statements together. Bonhoeffer's early talent was not fully developed, but he left us an example of a man who fulfilled his supreme calling by following Christ, even through death. May we too have the courage to die every day to our vocation, however difficult it may be.

Don't miss out!

Visit the website below and you can sign up to receive emails whenever Bible Sermons publishes a new book. There's no charge and no obligation.

https://books2read.com/r/B-A-MZBS-TVIHC

BOOKS 2 READ

Connecting independent readers to independent writers.

Did you love *God's Guide for Work: Discovering God's Will for a Particular Job*? Then you should read *Analyzing Labor Education in the Pentateuch and Books Historical*[1] by Bible Sermons!

[2]

Discover the work principles and wisdom found in the Pentateuch and Historical Books of the Bible! This fundamental work will help you understand the origins of a renewed work ethic and the importance of being a diligent worker. Through this book you will understand the work lessons of biblical characters, find compelling examples of people who were blessed by being proactive, and gain vital strategies for

---

1. https://books2read.com/u/bwyGMZ

2. https://books2read.com/u/bwyGMZ

putting these concepts into practice. *Be the best worker you can be with the Pentateuch and Historical Books of the Bible!*

Also by Bible Sermons

Notes in the New Testament

Analyzing Notes in the Book of Matthew: Fulfillments of Old Testament Prophecies

Analyzing Notes in the Book of Mark: Finding Peace in Difficult Times

Analyzing Notes in the Book of Luke: The Divine Love of Jesus Revealed

Analyzing Notes in the Book of John: John's Contribution to the New Testament Scriptures

Analyzing Notes in the Book of the Acts of the Apostles: A Journey of Continuation in the Work of Jesus

Overflying The Bible

Bible Introduction: Overflying The Bible from Genesis by Brethren in the Faith

Chronological Prophecy: Things That Will Happen on Earth

Bible Study: Genesis 1. Creation in Six Days

The Education of Labor in the Bible

Analyzing the Education of Labor in Genesis: The Purpose of Life on Earth

Analyzing the Teaching of Labor in Exodus: From Slavery to Liberation

Analyzing the Labor Education in Leviticus: The Spirit of the Law at Work

Analyzing the Labor Education in Numbers: Israel's Desert Experience for Today's Challenges

Analyzing the Labor Education in Deuteronomy: A Perspective on Working Life Today

Analyzing Labor Education in Joshua and Judges: Motivation for Hard work!

Analyzing Labor Education in Ruth: A Reference for Self-growth and Self-improvement

Analyzing Labor Education in Samuel, kings and Chronicles: A Study of Leadership in Antiquity

Analyzing Labor Education in Ezra, Nehemiah, Esther: A Look at the Past to Orient our Future Work

Analyzing Labor Education in Job: Spiritual and Professional Example for Working Life

Analyzing Labor Education in Psalms: Ethics, Works and Words

Analyzing Labor Education in Pentateuch

Analyzing Labor Education in the Historical Books: Applying the Bible to Practical Labor

Analyzing Labor Education in the Pentateuch and Books Historical

God's Guide for Work: Discovering God's Will for a Particular Job

Standalone
Analyzing Notes in the 4 Gospels: Commentary Biblical
Analyzing What is to Come: God's Prophecies

About the Author

This bible study series is perfect for Christians of any level, from children to youth to adults. It provides an engaging and interactive way to learn the Bible, with activities and discussion topics that will help deepen your understanding of scripture and strengthen your faith. Whether you're a beginner or an experienced Christian, this series will help you grow in your knowledge of the Bible and strengthen your relationship with God. Led by brothers with exemplary testimonies and extensive knowledge of scripture, who congregate in the name of the Lord Jesus Christ throughout the world.

About the Publisher

Editor

Elvis A. Betancourt T. 4135 Stoney Creek Dr., Lincolnton, NC 28092 *elvisbetancourtt@gmail.com*

Contáctenos

Preguntas y comentarios generales: *seminitt25@gmail.com*